The Society of Friends

by
George H. Gorman

FOREWORD BY
GERALD PRIESTLAND

D0996148

THE RELIGIOUS EDUCATION PRESS
A Division of Pergamon Press

A. Wheaton & Company Limited
A Division of Pergamon Press
Hennock Road, Exeter EX2 8RP

Pergamon Press Ltd
Headington Hill Hall, Oxford OX3 0BW

Pergamon Press Inc.
Maxwell House, Fairview Park, Elmsford,
New York 10523

Pergamon of Canada Ltd
75 The East Mall, Toronto, Ontario M8Z 2L9

Pergamon Press (Australia) Pty Ltd
19a Boundary Street, Rushcutters Bay, N.S.W. 2011

Pergamon Press GmbH
6242 Kronberg/Taunus, Pferdstrasse 1,
Frankfurt-am-Main, West Germany

First edition 1978
Reprinted 1978

Printed in Great Britain by A. Wheaton & Co. Ltd, Exeter
ISBN 0 08 021412 6 flexi net
ISBN 0 08 021411 8 flexi non net

Contents

ACKNOWLEDGEMENTS

Thanks are due to the following for permission to reproduce photographs: Society of Friends (pages 9, 20, 21, 29, 40, 48, 53, 58) and the Ironbridge Gorge Museum Trust (page 35).

COVER PHOTOGRAPH: *Friends gather for coffee after a meeting at Cirencester Meeting House.*

Foreword

Not long ago a reporter took his microphone into the street and asked people what they knew about the Quakers. Most of them said 'Porridge', but one added 'Mean little men in black hats with gloomy faces'.

George Gorman may be little by my standards (I am six feet seven), but I know he isn't mean or gloomy, and I don't think he owns a hat at all. He is in fact a rather jolly man who smokes a pipe and acts as a sort of universal uncle to British Friends.

George certainly helped to convince me that you don't have to be mean or miserable to be a Friend. Nor do you have to be superhumanly good, either. George helped me discover that Friends are ordinary everyday people who get on with life without moaning about sin and virtue all the time. Even someone like me could be a Friend – actually *was* a Friend. For you don't get converted into a Quaker; you gradually come to realise that you *are* one, usually because other Friends start treating you as one.

What does being a Quaker mean to me? It means my work and my faith, my everyday life and my religious life, are all one. It means listening for God, waiting on him – not lecturing and pestering him, telling him what he already knows or what he ought to be doing for us. It means quietness (which is a blessing in a profession like mine). It means a constant searching after the truth; for surely God did not say his last word to Man with the final full stop of the Bible? It means active peacemaking and non-violence. It means a rather fascinating way of reaching group decisions, without scoring points or winning votes. It means real friendship; it means equality of sex and race; and it means having a tradition of many fine men and women behind you. Even if some of them did wear black hats.

Gerald Priestland

1

A
Friends
Meeting

The Society of Friends is sometimes described as a 'do-it-yourself religion'. This is because there are no priests or ministers to whom members can look for leadership. Nor are members asked to accept creeds or dogmatic statements of faith which they may not understand or even believe sincerely. Basically Friends are people who like to think for themselves, and they usually hold strong religious convictions. While they like to stand on their own feet, they know that within the Society they can help each other to discover the truth about life. They will also find the love that gives them the courage to live as real people.

The easiest way to give a picture of the Society of Friends as it is today is to describe what a Quaker Meeting is like. The one I'm going to write about is my own meeting at Winchmore Hill, which is some ten miles from the centre of London. It meets in a pleasant Meeting House, which was built in 1799 (there was an earlier building, erected about 1688, but it fell down!). The main meeting room is oblong in shape. The walls are panelled with wood to about half way up and the rest is painted white. There are several large windows, and the general effect is of a bright, cheerful, simple room.

The seating consists mostly of wooden benches arranged in an open square facing inwards. In the centre is a table on which are two or three books including a Bible. There are generally some flowers.

Every Sunday morning just before 10.30 people begin to arrive at the Meeting House. Among the first will be the Friend (man or woman) who is acting as 'doorkeeper' for the day. His job is to greet people as they arrive, with a special welcome for any visitor who is coming for the first time. People may sit anywhere they wish, although most of the regulars have their favourite spots.

THE MEETING   The actual Meeting for Worship starts when the first Friend arrives and sits down in silence. Others come in and join him, and soon after 10.30 about forty or fifty people, including children, will have taken their places. All have entered the room quietly and there is a lovely sense of stillness, which is a great contrast to the general racket of modern life. Even quite young children seem to enjoy the peace, although they may chatter a bit. This worries their parents, but no one else minds; in fact most people rather like it. After about fifteen minutes the young children leave the meeting and go to other rooms, but we will forget them for the moment.

As I have just said, the Quaker meeting starts in silence, and sometimes nothing will be said for the whole hour that a meeting normally lasts. Usually after a fairly long opening period of quiet, someone, man or woman, boy or girl, will feel that he or she has an experience that will help the other people present. It could be something that has happened during the week, or something they have read. Or they will recall a passage from the Bible, or a poem that has taken on a new meaning. The purpose of speaking, reading or praying out loud in meeting is to express what

A Meeting for Worship in session.

the speaker feels is happening deep in the silence in which they are all meeting. The object of speaking is to help everyone to be even more aware of their links with one another. Whatever is said should be the sincere experience of the speaker. It will be received in silence, and will help to make the silence itself more profound.

During the hour of the meeting possibly three or four people may speak. Discussion and argument are quite out of place. Friends call spoken contributions 'ministry', and at their best they will blend together to make a whole. Often what someone says will express vividly a vague idea that has been forming in my mind. Sometimes the pattern that emerges is so clear that you would think that the speakers must have got together to plan what they will say. It is difficult to realise that the ministry is spontaneous. This is all the more remarkable as we do not sing hymns or use a prayer book, or have any kind of programme for a service, not even a sermon.

The time for closing the meeting makes itself felt quite naturally by a gentle restlessness among those present. The meeting is formally ended by two Friends (whom we call Elders) shaking hands. Nowadays most people present will also shake hands with the persons sitting next to them.

What I have written so far about a Meeting for Worship may well seem to many of my readers to be nothing like what they think of as proper worship. So I will try to explain it by describing what has been going on in the minds of those present. In fact the best way of doing this is to tell you the kind of thing that happens to me in meeting. In common with everyone else, having taken my place, I try to be as relaxed as possible. Sitting on a bench may not sound very comfortable, but it is. The actual ways in which I start meeting cán vary quite a bit. Though we start as individuals, what we are all trying to do is to draw very close to one another in spirit.

Sometimes I may be trying to sort out the meaning of something that has happened to me recently. Perhaps my pride was hurt by someone. As I sit in meeting I recall the angry resentment I felt. But as the silence surrounds me I begin to wonder whether I was right to be so annoyed, and also whether I should not try to do something to put things right between us. I slowly realise that my state of anger contradicts my basic conviction that God is love, and that I should try to act in a loving way towards people.

At other times meeting starts for me when I remember a film I've seen, or something on television which has caught my attention. I ask myself: 'How does that idea fit into the view of the world as a place where loving people is the most important thing we can do?'

Yet another point of departure could be to lock my attention on to a saying of Jesus or some other great religious teacher – not so much thinking about it as being absorbed by it. The technical term for this is 'meditation'. Or perhaps I may find myself just thinking about someone who has reason to be very happy, or alternatively someone who is ill, depressed or just miserable. By thinking about them in the special silence of the meeting I may share their joy or their sorrow, and help them to be aware of the fact that God loves them. The technical term for this is 'prayer'.

Of course quite often I arrive at meeting in a rather vague state of mind, and I gently drift through the hour like this. It is a pleasant, relaxed and extremely refreshing experience. Although nothing very 'religious' seems to have happened, on looking back I know that I have been supported by the love of my friends, and through this I have known what we speak of as the love of God.

BEING TOGETHER   I spoke above of a 'point of departure'. To depart means moving away from where I was. But I have also said that I'm sitting on a bench–so where am I moving to? What I and the others present are doing is starting out on a mental journey. The best way of imagining this is to think of going down deep into your inner self. This is quite natural language to use, for when we think really hard about something we say 'I thought deeply about that'. When people fall in love, we say they are 'deeply in love'.

So I and all the others in the room, in a great variety of ways, have been making a 'spiritual' journey to the deepest parts of ourselves. All sorts of exciting things can happen as we do this. We may relive the experience of some happy event that brought us joy, and made a lot of difference to our lives. But, equally, we may remember something quite ghastly which still has the power to make us afraid. When this happens to me I recall what a member of my meeting told me of the way she often started her inward journey. She said: 'I look around the room and think how marvellous it is that so many people here love me and I love them.' So, if I'm afraid of what I find on my journey inwards, I look at some of the people near me and know the truth of the words of the New Testament that 'perfect love casts out fear'.

Here the silence of the meeting is a tremendous help, because gradually you find that you are in communication with all the people in the room, although nothing has been said. This is not as strange as it sounds, if you think about your own particular friends. When you share some dramatic experience with them you may not be able to find the right words to say. In being silent together you find that you have expressed joy, understanding or sympathy in a better way than you could have done by speaking.

What Friends have known for over three hundred years is that when people make the kind of experimental journey I have described, sooner or later they reach a quiet place in the still centre of their lives. This actually happens in Meeting for Worship, sometimes quite quickly, sometimes more slowly. Early Friends talked about this as 'centring down'. When you get used to the way of silent worship you can often tell when, to use another old phrase, 'the meeting was truly gathered'. In modern words what has happened is that the individuals in the room have made their journey to the centre of their real selves. When they reach this quiet place two things happen at the same time. Everyone knows, firstly, that he or she is a unique, individual person; and secondly that each person present is unable to be truly himself or herself, without the help of others.

While remaining individuals, at the same time all the people in the meeting have become one group. They are now a team working towards a common goal. That goal was well expressed by Robert Barclay (1648–90) who joined the Society in its early years. He wrote these words of his first experience of Friends' worship '... when I came into the silent assemblies of God's people, I felt a secret power among them, which touched my heart; and as I gave way unto it I found the evil weakening in me and the good raised up'.

Modern Friends would warmly agree with Robert Barclay that the power which touched his heart in meeting was the power of the love of God. It is this love that is present in the spirit of all real Meetings for Worship. It binds all who are there into a loving, caring group. Being loved helps people to become more loving. So they do not feel so guilty about the nastier sides of their nature which are changed by being in the presence of the love of God. Meeting for Worship is also a time when we can pay special attention to the most important things in life such as love, beauty, truth and goodness, and so allow them to influence our lives. For these are the values by which Jesus lived.

But a Meeting for Worship only makes sense when people discover for themselves something of the love of God, and of the meaning and purpose of life, and then express it in good actions in everyday life. This becomes obvious after the close of the meeting. Its secretary (Friends call the holder of this office the Clerk) first warmly welcomes any visitors, and then gives out the notices of events the Meeting is organising. Attention is called to any action the Society of Friends may be taking locally or nationally. This could be social work in this country or overseas, or other things Friends would be interested in such as Oxfam, Shelter or Help the Aged.

Once the notices are over everyone seems to be talking to everyone else, and the children reappear, bringing with them the work that they have been doing. It is in this social time, when coffee is often served, that you find out what a variety of people have been present. We have a number of teachers, social workers, two or three doctors and a few people involved in other medical work. There are always a fair number of housewives, people in business, a journalist, a carpenter and some who work in factories. There are generally a number of students and others who are at school. To round off the whole, there are some men and women who have retired from work but certainly not from life.

Despite the popular view that Friends are rigid puritans 'who say No to everything from whist to war', these people

13

are normal, happy and cheerful human beings. All of them aim to carry the sense of peace and purpose they have found in meeting into everyday life. They may often fail to do this but at least they will try. The clothes they wear tend to be casual rather than formal – and they are quite unlike those worn by the chap on the porridge packet!

The attempt to live in a loving, truthful way brings great satisfaction, but it can also be hard work. It often seems easier to ignore the truth about difficult problems like war, racial hatred and poverty. Because Friends respect the life and teaching of Jesus, and believe that religion affects every aspect of life, they feel they must continually try to find answers to such evils.

In their quiet Meetings for Worship they discover a source of love and power that helps them to face life with the conviction that it is basically good. The experience of George Fox in the seventeenth century is our starting-point. If any one person can be described as the founder of the Society of Friends, it must be Fox. We know a great deal about what he did and thought because he wrote many letters and some books, the most famous of his writings being *The Journal of George Fox*.

Think about . . .

What are the advantages and disadvantages of having or not having priests and ministers?

Can you recall a situation in which something wonderful or dreadful has happened to you and your friends, which has been impossible to talk about and yet in silence you have been able to communicate your deepest feelings?

In what ways do you think meditation can help people to explore some of their deepest experiences?

2

How Quakers Began

Climbing Pendle Hill was hard work. The smooth grass was slippery on the steep hillside, making it difficult for George Fox to get a foothold. The only way of getting up was to use the sheep tracks.

It was a sweltering day in May 1652. Fox was hot and sticky in his doublet and leather breeches. These were hard wearing, and fine for riding horses, but not for struggling up a steep hill.

But he must get to the top. The urge to climb had gripped him as soon as he saw Pendle Hill dominating the Lancashire countryside. Now he was almost at the top: he pushed back his white hat and wiped the sweat from his face. One final effort and he was there.

The going was easier on the wide bleak moorland which still sloped gently upwards, and George was able to think about what he was doing. He was a powerfully built man of twenty-eight. For the last nine years he had been travelling on horse or on foot all over England. Everywhere he went he felt he must try to free people from the dry, dull way in which they lived. The churches of his day seemed unable to help them, and had certainly not been of much use to him.

As he came to the highest point of the hill a wonderful view stretched before him, for miles around and away to the Irish Sea in the distance. As he watched it seemed to him that in the valleys below there were many people, ready to be gathered together to form a living church, not brick and stone buildings, but a church made up of people who had found the reality of God in their own experience.

So powerful was his feeling that he found himself shouting out loud that this was the 'Day of the Lord'. For he felt this was the day when ordinary people could discover for themselves what the life and teaching of Jesus really meant. Fox knew that from now on he must try to gather together those who were willing to be influenced by the living spirit of Jesus into a movement which God could use to change the whole nation. His ambition may seem presumptuous and even arrogant, but he was a young man filled with overwhelming zeal.

George ran down the hillside and mounted his horse. As he rode off he thought back over his life, and how he had come to feel as he did now.

A SEARCH FOR TRUTH   He remembered his parents: his father, Christopher Fox, was a weaver and churchwarden of Fenny Drayton, the Leicestershire village where George was born in July 1624. The villagers nicknamed his father 'righteous Christer' because of his fine character. His mother came from a family who had been persecuted for their religious views.

Yes, his parents were good people, but they had not been able to satisfy the sense of longing George experienced deep inside himself. They had wanted him to be a clergyman, for he was interested in religious questions, but George knew this was not for him.

Instead he went to work for a year or so with a local

dealer, who made shoes and kept cattle and sheep. On Sundays, when other people were in church, George wandered in the fields reading the Bible, and came to know a lot of it by heart. He liked his job, especially looking after the sheep, as this gave him the chance to be quiet and to think.

Then he recalled the day when as part of his work he had gone to a fair with two of his cousins, to help in buying some goods for his master's shop. After they had done their business they invited George to the local inn for a drink. Marketing was thirsty work so he joined them. He knew his cousins were Puritans—religious men who wanted to purify religion. So George was all the more shocked to discover that, having quenched their thirst, they continued drinking on the understanding that the first of them to go under the table would pay for the lot!

As soon as he realised what was happening, George paid for his drink and left the inn. He felt terribly depressed. How, he asked himself, could good people behave so badly? Why did their beliefs have so little effect on the way they lived?

For the next few weeks he pestered everyone with his questions. He asked his family, his friends, and many of the parsons in the district, but none could give him a satisfactory reply. Finally he knew he must leave home, although he loved his parents and they loved him, and seek an answer elsewhere.

So in 1643, when he was nineteen, George started on his travels. Life was not easy and he often slept rough in haystacks and under hedges. He met many people and questioned them about their beliefs. Some were gentle and kind, but many refused to take him seriously and could not understand what troubled him.

THE GREAT DISCOVERY   After some months, he had begun to feel lonely and hopeless. Life seemed to have no purpose, and no one had been able to help him. Then suddenly something happened. He seemed to hear an inner voice which said, 'There is one even Christ Jesus who can speak to thy condition.' This made his 'heart leap for joy'. This was his way of saying that at last he had found an answer – the life and teaching of Jesus really were important to him.

The effect on him was tremendous. Fox knew that true religion could completely change his outlook on life. It was so different from the dull, dry, formal attitudes held by many people. It was not even doing things like going to church services, singing psalms, reciting creeds and repeating prayers. It was something that had happened deep inside himself. God was not far away from people but actually present in their deepest experience – there was something of God in everyone.

George Fox returned to his village and stayed with his parents for a short while. But he knew he couldn't stop with them. He must share his exciting discovery with as many people as possible. So he set off on his travels again, this time driven by the sense that he must try to help people to discover God within themselves. For this would release them from their inner fears and enable them to live more vitally, full of the courage to love God and other people.

He went from town to town and from village to village, telling everyone he met of the wonderful thing that had happened to him, making it clear that it could happen to them, too. He constantly pointed out that the truth of religion was its inner meaning – this, not its outward form of church-going, was the important thing. Through it people could find God in a way that would completely transform the way they lived, and their behaviour towards others.

George was not always tactful in the way he spoke, for he felt very strongly. He called churches 'steeple houses', and described clergymen as 'hireling [hired] priests', for they accepted payment for preaching the gospel – the good news about God – which Fox believed should be freely shared with all.

While many were convinced of the truth of what Fox

said, others were angry with him for his direct challenging of the things they valued. So he was frequently attacked with great violence, and was beaten and had stones thrown at him. By the time he climbed Pendle Hill he had twice been put in prison for what his opponents considered to be blasphemy. Thoughts like these may well have been in his mind as he rode away from Pendle Hill.

THE BIRTH OF THE SOCIETY   He made his way north and a few days later, on Whit Sunday, he came to Firbank Fell, some thirty miles from Pendle. Word had got around that a fiery young preacher had arrived in the district, and about a thousand people gathered to hear him. Standing in the open on a large rock, still known as Fox's Pulpit, George spoke to the crowd for about three hours, telling them of his discovery.

Many of those who listened to Fox that day felt much the same way about life as he did. Like him they were dissatisfied with their churches: they were seeking for a religion that was real. It seemed to them that lots of people who claimed to believe in God were hypocrites – they didn't practise their religion in their daily lives. Others were sincere enough, but they held a lot of complicated beliefs that didn't seem to ring true to life.

On that Sunday in 1652 many hundreds were convinced of the truth of what George Fox said. Although he did not realise it at the time, the Quaker movement had begun. Fox was a natural leader and organiser, but there were also a number of other men and women who shared these gifts as well as his convictions. Together they set about the task of drawing together those who were attracted to this new attitude to religion, and uniting themselves into an informal society in which they could care for and support one another. They did not want to call it a 'church' because they were so disillusioned with the churches of their day. So they spoke of themselves as 'Friends of Truth', or the 'Children of the Light', or just simply as 'Friends'. They talked of 'the light' because it now filled their lives which had once seemed full of darkness.

To the people of their time these first Friends did not seem at all like a proper church. They had no priests or parsons; among the Friends of Truth everyone was equal, and even women were allowed to take part in their services, a thing almost unheard of in those days. Friends disliked creeds, doctrine and dogma, calling them 'notions' and thinking of them as a substitute for religion. Their way of worship was also unlike the usual church service, for Friends just sat still and quiet together.

Friends stood out from their fellows in the way in which they spoke to people. In the seventeenth century if you thought someone was your social equal or superior you addressed him with the plural pronoun 'you'. When you spoke to those you considered your inferiors you called them 'thee' or 'thou'. Friends believed that all people were

The old Meeting House at Come-to-Good in Cornwall.

A new Meeting House: Wanstead.

equal, and so to get over the problem of dividing people into social classes they said 'thee' and 'thou' to everyone. When George Fox wrote to Oliver Cromwell, he started his letter 'Dear Friend', and went on 'Be still . . . and that will give thee wisdom. . . .' Later when Fox met Cromwell he refused to take off his hat. Keeping their hats on was another way in which Friends witnessed to equality.

THE PERSECUTIONS   People get extremely angry when social customs are not observed. Because of their protests against conventions, the first Friends were bitterly persecuted just as George Fox had been during his early travels. It was always easy to make trouble for Friends, because they refused to swear an oath of loyalty to the state, or in a court of law. They believed that people should be trusted, and should always speak the truth. So to get a Friend into prison all you had to do was to ask him to take the oath. Friends also objected to paying tithes – taxes for the upkeep of the Church which they believed to be false.

Thousands of Friends went to prison for these and other reasons. While they used every legal method to avoid going to gaol they never responded to violence by being violent themselves. Instead they tried to answer 'that of God' in those who persecuted them. By an Act of Parliament only services in the recognised Church were allowed, but Friends defied this law, and continued to hold their own quiet meetings for worship.

Persecution was specially strong at Reading where, in the ten years before the granting of a general pardon in 1672, most of the Friends were in prison at some time or other. Sunday, 11 January 1662 was typical of what happened during the whole long period. On that day the whole meeting was 'pulled out of the house' in which Friends had gathered for worship – but the following Sunday they were back again.

Eight years later, in 1670, the Reading Friends were still being persecuted. In that year all the men and women were in prison most of the time, so the meeting was maintained on many Sundays by the 'children and young maidens'. In an attempt to break the spirit of the Quakers the Justice and Constable, on several Sundays, had buckets of water thrown over the worshippers. On one occasion they ordered that the benches on which Friends sat should be chopped up.

During the period of sustained attack we know that six Reading Friends died in prison, and there is at least one record of a child being struck while Friends were being driven from their meeting. Despite all this, Friends always held their meetings in the town, apart from the one or two times when everyone was in prison. Then the new prisoners shared in the Meetings for Worship regularly held by the Friends already there.

A NEW PEACE   It was this non-violent behaviour, which was a direct outcome of Friends' religious convictions, that helped to bring to England the right of every man to worship God according to his conscience. It also showed Friends a new way of dealing with human wickedness and violence. The years of the Civil War and Restoration were full of strife at home and overseas. Friends were convinced that war was not only a senseless way of settling disputes, but also evil and cruel.

Friends were also convinced that to believe in the God of love of which the New Testament speaks, meant that they must behave in a loving manner to other people. But this is a difficult thing to do, and it clearly meant that they must try to love and trust others. So Friends needed to find the strength of character, will and purpose to achieve this way of life. They found this power in their quiet Meetings for Worship, which were similar to those that I have already described in the first chapter. In the seventeenth century, however, they often lasted for several hours and were sometimes held out of doors.

Several times the name 'Quaker' has crept into my writing as an alternative to 'Friend'. It was a mocking term used by people to make fun of the fact that the early Friends sometimes trembled or quaked in their Meetings for Worship, because they were so strongly awed by their sense of the presence of God. A magistrate, annoyed because Fox told the Justices of Derby to 'tremble at the word of God', replied by calling George and his friends 'Quakers'. Like most nicknames the term has stuck, and today members of the Society of Friends are better known as Quakers.

When George Fox died in 1691 at the age of sixty-seven, there were meetings of Friends all over the British Isles and many in America. He had fulfilled his vision on Pendle Hill to gather a people who would try to live in the loving spirit of Jesus. They found the strength to do this by worshipping quietly in silence, where they discovered God in themselves and in others.

A great deal of hard work and careful organisation was

required to achieve all this. The impact of the lives of Fox and his followers brought about some startling changes, and it still affects us today. In the following chapters we shall trace the links between the Society of Friends of George Fox's time and the Society today.

Think about . . .

Fox, like Wesley, travelled great distances on horseback to preach in towns and villages, mainly in the open air. (Consult his *Journal* to discover whether he visited your home town.) Why did these preachers feel it was essential for them to travel?

Do you think that many people today have a 'feeling' for religion but are reluctant to join a church? Would you be put off joining a church that had lots of traditions in services that you weren't familiar with? Do you think hymns and sermons are helpful, or do you find them mostly irrelevant to your everyday life?

Why do you think Fox and the early Friends were so bitterly persecuted? Was it sensible of them to respond in a non-violent way? Do you know of any places today where people are persecuted for their religious beliefs? Why do you think this is?

3

The Turbulent Years

Any manager of a modern football club can expect to have difficulties in persuading his star players to work together harmoniously. Stars are generally people with strong wills and when they are in a team there will inevitably be clashes of personality. Religious 'stars' are just as awkward to deal with, and the early Society of Friends attracted a considerable number of strong and powerful personalities. Part of the genius of George Fox was that he developed a simple, democratic organisation that allowed all Friends to share in the running of the Society. At the same time it prevented the growth of any small, powerful groups that could dominate the rest.

LEADERSHIP But Fox nearly fell into the power trap. One of the early Friends, James Nayler (1616–60), was a brilliant public speaker, and helped to 'convince' many people of the truth of Quaker ideas. He had a strong personal following in the south and west of England, whose flattery turned his head. Foolishly, on 24 October 1656,

Nayler was persuaded by them to ride into Bristol, with a group around his horse singing 'Holy, holy, holy, Lord God of Israel'. Women spread garments on the road before him. While Nayler's intention was undoubtedly innocent, his action deeply shocked the people of Bristol. To them it was blasphemous, and he and his party were arrested. Nayler was later brought to London and examined by a committee of the House of Commons. After a lengthy debate he was sentenced to have his tongue bored through, to be put in the pillory, and then to be publicly whipped through the streets of London and Bristol before being returned to prison.

Nayler suffered this terrible punishment without complaint, for he deeply regretted the harm that he had caused to the Society of Friends, which he loved and had tried to serve. Two hours before his death at the age of forty-four he spoke some beautiful words, of which the following is the opening sentence:

> There is a spirit which I feel that delights to do no evil, nor to revenge any wrong, but delights to endure all things, in hope to enjoy its own in the end. . . .

MONTHLY MEETINGS Fox and Nayler were clearly jealous and suspicious of each other, as rivals for the leadership of the Society. Had there been a better understanding between them it is possible that Nayler would have been able to avoid his extravagant behaviour. Fox was furious with him for exposing the young Society, which they had worked so hard to create, to such danger. There is no doubt that his difficulties with James Nayler warned Fox of the danger of too much power resting with any one person. It made him realise that some kind of organisation was needed, to help to control himself as well as the less stable elements in the Society.

So between 1667 and 1669 Fox travelled all over the country on horseback, though he was in great personal discomfort, for his joints were swollen and stiff after three years in prison. The purpose of his travels was to set up

'Monthly Meetings'. These gatherings, as their name implies, were held each month, and they drew together all the Friends in an area to make decisions about everything that affected the life of the Society in the locality. Power was thus spread among all those associated with the Society throughout the country. This system of running the Society, set up by George Fox over three hundred years ago, still functions satisfactorily today.

MARGARET FELL   Margaret Fell was a seventeenth-century Friend who did a lot to help the early enthusiastic groups of Friends to become well organised and so to survive as a Society of Friends. Judge Thomas Fell and his wife Margaret lived at Swarthmore Hall, near Ulverston, in Lancashire. It was to their home that George Fox and his friends went to stay after the great gathering on Firbank Fell. Margaret became a Quaker and brought gifts of common sense and practical loving care to the Society: in fact Swarthmore Hall was virtually its headquarters. This shows great tolerance on behalf of Judge Fell as, although he was sympathetic, he never became a Friend. He died in 1658.

Many of those who had become Quakers, as a result of hearing Fox and other Friends preach, felt a strong urge themselves to seek to spread the message of Quakerism. They travelled all over the country and many people gladly responded to what they had to say. But others reacted violently against these 'Publishers of Truth', as Quakers described them, and they had to endure great suffering and hardship.

Margaret Fell kept open house for them at Swarthmore Hall, to which they could return to rest between their travels. She also wrote them encouraging letters while they were away on their journeys. While they tried, as far as they could, to keep themselves, the money they could earn was limited. So Margaret Fell organised the 'Kendal Fund' to give them financial help, and also to assist the families that they had left at home.

These practical services would seem to be the limit that a woman with a large household could manage. But the remarkable Margaret Fell made two extended visits to London, lasting many months. Whilst she was there she took up with the King, and others in authority, the cases of Quakers who had been put in prison. Her efforts were not in vain. Though Charles II could not stop the persecution of Quakers, he did order the release of many Friends to celebrate his marriage in 1662. Margaret herself joined in the travels of Friends. In the summer of 1663, with her daughters Sarah and Mary, she set off on a trip of about a thousand miles to visit Quaker Meetings in England.

The fact that she was a woman did not keep Margaret Fell out of prison. In 1664 she was asked to promise Ulverston Magistrates that she would not hold any more Quaker meetings at Swarthmore Hall. When she refused to make such a promise she was asked to swear an oath of allegiance to the King. This she could not do because she felt that taking an oath was forbidden by the teaching of Jesus. So she was sent to prison in Lancaster Castle, where she remained for four years. After being allowed home for a short period she had to serve a further term of imprisonment from 1670 to 1671.

In 1669, eleven years after the death of Judge Fell, Margaret married George Fox. It must have been a strange marriage, as they were hardly ever together because of George's frequent travels. But the letters they sent to one another are deeply loving and affectionate. Margaret Fell died in 1702, aged eighty-eight.

WILLIAM PENN   Another powerful personality who became a Quaker in the early years of the Society was William Penn (1644–1718). He was the son of an admiral, and his father was terribly upset when, in 1667, William threw in his lot with the despised Quakers. Readers will recall that Quakers felt that fighting was the wrong way to try to settle disputes: many of them had been in the Civil War and

Penn trading with the Indians.

knew how cruel, wicked and senseless it was. As a courtier young William Penn was in the habit of wearing a sword. It is said that after he had been a Quaker for some time he asked George Fox for his advice about this. Fox replied, 'Wear it as long as thou canst!' – in other words, 'as long as your conscience will let you'. The story goes that soon after this conversation William got rid of his sword.

Like most of the first Friends, Penn found himself in prison several times during his life. His trial at the Old Bailey in 1670 has become famous because it established the right of a jury to bring in its verdict according to conscience and not to the dictates of those in authority.

William Penn and another Quaker, William Mead, were accused of causing a riot in Gracechurch Street in the City of London. The Quakers were forced to meet in the road because the authorities had locked them out of their Meeting House, after a law was passed to prevent religious freedom. The Recorder of London – a senior Judge – told the jury to find Penn and Mead guilty. But Penn urged the jury not to convict them, because he felt that they were innocent. The jury angered the Judge by merely finding Penn 'guilty of speaking in Gracious [Gracechurch] Street', which was not a crime. They found Mead 'not guilty'. The Judge immediately had the jury locked up and refused to free them until they brought in the verdict he wanted. But the jury stood their ground, thanks largely to the influence and bravery of their foreman, Edward Bushell. After many weeks of struggle their verdict was accepted, and both the jury and the two Quakers were freed.

In 1681 Charles II gave a large area of land in the American colonies to William Penn, in settlement of a debt of £16 000 that Charles I had owed to William's father Admiral Penn. There was some discussion about the name to be given to the territory. As the land was known to be heavily wooded the King insisted that it should be called Penn-sylvania; Penn in honour of the dead admiral, and sylvania from the Latin word for a wood.

It was an opportunity for William Penn to put into practice his ideas for running a state on the Christian principles of love, justice and freedom. It was to be his 'holy experiment', where people could practise their religious ideas without fear of persecution. Many Quakers, exhausted by their suffering in Britain, crossed the Atlantic to start a new life in Philadelphia – the city of 'brotherly love', and in the beautiful country that surrounded it.

One of Penn's major concerns was to establish good relations with the native Indians. He made a treaty with them which guaranteed, among other things, that land would be purchased from them at a fair price. Although the Indians often responded with violence to the bad treatment they received from other settlers, they never did any harm to the Quakers who came to live among them. The 'holy experiment' was remarkably successful while the Quakers formed the government of Pennsylvania.

Among William Penn's many gifts were those of a writer. He joined with vigour in the wordy battle that went on between the various Christian groups of his day, using his pen to promote and defend Quaker ideas. One of his most remarkable books was an *Essay Towards the Present and Future Peace of Europe*. In this he foreshadowed the forming of the European Community. One of his early books, *No Cross, No Crown*, was written while he was in prison in the Tower of London.

In this chapter every Quaker I have named spent time in prison. Their imprisonment was caused by several Acts of Parliament aimed at suppressing religious freedom. Quaker Meetings and any refusal to take an Oath were made illegal by the Quaker Act of 1662. The Conventicle Acts of 1664 and 1670 made any religious meetings other than those of the Church of England illegal, and the Five Mile Act forbade all ministers, who did not accept the Church of England, to teach in schools or live within five miles of a town.

In the twenty-year period before the Act of Toleration (1689) it is estimated that 12 000 Quakers suffered imprisonment, and more than 300 died in captivity. Yet throughout this period Quakers continued to hold their quiet Meetings for Worship. They could follow no other course because they believed so strongly that they must be able to worship God in a way they passionately believed to be right.

Because Friends spent so much of their time in prison they knew of the awful state of these places in seventeenth-century Britain. They were constantly urging the local Justices to improve conditions, not so much for themselves as for their fellow prisoners. So started the Quaker interest in penal reform and their concern for human freedom, which for them were all part of their religious life. This remains true of the Society today.

Think about . . .

How can any society be organised so as to get the best out of the members, but prevent powerful personalities from dominating the rest?

Is it important that responsibility for making decisions should be shared among all the members of a church? Or is it better to appoint leaders to make decisions and to deal with administration?

Can you imagine anyone setting up a 'holy experiment' today? (Think of some of the religious communes set up by ordinary people.) Now that persecution has stopped, would it be worth doing, or is it more important to live out your beliefs in the ordinary world?

4

The Quaker Way of Life

It is not surprising, after the battering that Friends took in the first fifty years of the Society, that they were quite happy to enjoy a more peaceful existence from the turn of the century.

From about 1700 for the next hundred years or so the Society entered its so-called 'Quietest Period'. However, do not be confused by this term. Life for Quakers was certainly quieter than in the turbulent years of the seventeenth century, but Friends were not less active although their energies were expressed in different ways.

Quaker principles encouraged Friends to adopt a simple life-style, and discouraged them from earning their living by engaging in luxury trades. The ancient universities would not admit anyone who was not a member of the Church of England, so Friends had to find new outlets for their energies. Here their religious conviction that God was to be discovered in every aspect of life was a great help to them, for it prevented them from making a sharp division between things thought to be 'holy' and those thought to be ordinary.

For Quakers life was a whole and could not be divided up – so God could be found in the work you did day by day, just as he could be discovered in Meeting for Worship.

QUAKERS IN INDUSTRY If this sounds like pious talk, let us see how it works out in the lives of particular Quakers whose attitudes were typical of Friends of the time. The first example is the story of the iron works at Coalbrookdale in Shropshire. Abraham Darby's family had long been interested in dealing with iron as blacksmiths. Because they were willing to experiment with new ways of working the metal, their business rapidly expanded.

In 1708 Abraham, a Quaker, became the manager of the iron works at Coalbrookdale, which is about eight miles from Bridgnorth. Here he had already developed a new process of smelting iron with coke, and so began a fresh epoch in the manufacture of iron. He also invented a method of casting 'iron-bellied pots' – pots which were wider in the middle than at the top and bottom. One of the many benefits of his firm's work was to produce a wide range of cast-iron household goods that could be bought at reasonable prices by poorer people.

Another important step forward taken some years later by the Darby family, was the manufacture of cast-iron cylinders for steam engines. By then another Quaker, Richard Reynolds, was manager – he had married Hannah Darby. Richard was a most inventive man, and thought up the idea of making cast-iron rails to replace the wooden ones of the works' railway. This was used for bringing coal and stores to the works from the River Severn, and the weight of the loads caused the wooden rails to break quite frequently.

The best-known product of the works was the Iron Bridge over the River Severn. Abraham Darby, the son of the founder of the firm, realised the inconvenience caused to people by the fact that they had to take a ferry every time they wanted to cross the river. So an iron bridge

The Iron Bridge.

was cast in the works. It was a massive structure, and when all the parts were assembled it weighed 387 tons. It was built between 1777 and 1779, and was the first of its kind in the world. It is still in use today, but for pedestrians only.

The Darby family felt that it was an essential part of their religious life to provide a works estate with adequate cottages for their workmen. There was no housing shortage, and comfortable dwellings were also available for the 'old and distressed persons'. In the course of the years, one day school and two Sunday schools were provided. Parks were set out in the neighbourhood for the use of the workmen and their families.

On Sundays the furnaces were shut down despite the technical disadvantages of doing this; the managers would rather lose something of their product 'than trespass on the right of their work people to have a free day for worship and leisure'.

There is no evidence of bickering over wages. During periods when food costs were high or there were severe shortages, the Darbys purchased flour, rice and grain and sold them to their workers at or below cost price.

When iron prices soared unjustly because of the American wars, the Darbys asked their customers, in the light of what they knew of the cost of material and labour, to fix what they considered to be a fair price. This was accepted by the firm without debate or question, though it was less than they could have obtained on the open market.

The family certainly made a lot of money, but they did not use it to make themselves grand. The Darby and Reynolds families remained plain simple Friends, believing that they were trustees of the wealth they had, which was to be used for the benefit of the poor and needy. They could quite certainly have made more money, had they been willing to take part in the lucrative arms trade, but this would have been entirely contrary to the religious beliefs they held.

All the managers of the firm from 1708 to 1791, and their families, were active members of the Society of Friends. The proper running of the iron works and the care of the people they employed, were to the Darby and the Reynolds families a natural part of the way they expressed their religious views.

Many other Friends became involved in industry and the names of the firms they started have become household names. Among the best known are the chocolate makers, Fry, Cadbury and Rowntree. Equally well known are Carrs, Jacobs and Huntley and Palmer who manufacture biscuits. Quakers were also responsible for Reckett's Blue and *Bradshaw's Railway Guide*. Banking was another area in which Quakers were concerned, and Barclays and Lloyds both have Quaker origins.

Strangely enough Friends are not responsible for Quaker Oats, the porridge. The name Quaker has often been used as a brand name, especially in America, for it was felt that the reputation Quakers had for quality would act as a guarantee of excellence. Many of the firms mentioned above are now public companies and the Quaker interest in them is, at most, minimal, although we like to think that they still recall their Quaker past with its concern for their employees and the quality of their goods and services.

A QUAKER AND SLAVERY   The Quaker concern to express religion in daily life was never better demonstrated than by the American Friend John Woolman (1720–72). As a young man working in a store he had to draw up a bill of sale for a black slave who had been purchased by a Quaker lady. Although Woolman knew that this lady would treat the negro well, he still felt uneasy, and told his employer that slave keeping was inconsistent with the Christian religion. He finally refused to have anything to do with transactions involving slaves.

As part of his Quaker activities Woolman undertook several long journeys to Friends in other parts of America. He stayed in wealthy Quaker homes where slaves were owned. This always made him feel extremely uneasy, but he never shirked the difficult task of expressing to the owners his views about the wrongness of keeping slaves. He had such a sensitive spirit that he was able to speak gently but firmly in a way that did not arouse antagonism.

But John Woolman was not content with words alone. He refused to wear dyed clothes because the dyes were made by slaves in the West Indies. He disliked looking peculiar, but he felt he must put up with this in order to witness to the evils of slavery. It was largely through Woolman's persistence that those American Quakers who kept slaves finally set them free.

John Woolman also felt a particular interest in the native Indians. The good relationships of William Penn's days had not been maintained, and many settlers had cheated the Indians and driven them from their traditional hunting grounds. The Indians retaliated by fighting and by scalping white settlers and soldiers. When bitter feelings were at their highest, Woolman made a long journey to visit the Indians in their own homes in order 'that I might understand their life and the spirit they live in, haply I might receive some instruction from them'. After travelling for eleven days he reached the Indian settlement at Wyalusing. During the next four days he had meetings with Chief Papunahung and his Indians, and he spoke of his recognition of the injustices the white men had done to the Indians. On the last day Woolman spoke and prayed so fervently that the interpreter could not keep up with him. But the Chief understood the spirit in which he was speaking. 'I love to hear where words come from,' he said.

In May 1772 Woolman set out on what was to be his last journey. He sailed 'steerage' to England, and during the thirty-nine days of the voyage had ample opportunity to discover how terrible were the conditions in which sailors had to work. On arrival in London he went to the annual gathering of senior Friends, where he handed in his certificate from Philadelphia Quakers testifying that he was a Quaker in good esteem among them. But he looked so strange, in his undyed clothes and uncured leather shoes, that one of the leading Friends present suggested that he had better return to America. John Woolman sat quietly for a time and then spoke. The Friends quickly recognised that Woolman was not a crank, but a quite outstanding person.

After Yearly Meeting Woolman travelled north, going on foot because he felt that the horses that pulled the stagecoaches were driven too hard. He reached York in September, when he was able to visit Friends. But he was already ill with smallpox and died a few days later.

During his life, with great sensitivity of spirit, he had constantly demonstrated his care for the poor whites, the

Indians and the Negro slaves. He had also been able to show his love for rich people who, he believed, harmed themselves by their exploitation of others.

A QUAKER AND PRISON WORK   One of the best known of all Quakers is Elizabeth Fry (1780–1845). Like John Woolman she felt a natural sympathy for people who suffered and, like him, was determined to do something about it. Her strong desire to help the victims of bad conditions made her take an interest in a variety of causes, but her chief work was with prisoners.

While a French Friend, Stephen Grellet, was visiting London he went to Newgate Prison, and was appalled by the state of the women's sick room.

> I was astonished beyond description at the mass of woe and misery I beheld. I found many sick, lying on the bare floor or on some old straw, having very scanty covering on them though it was quite cold; and there were several children born in the prison amongst them, almost naked. . . .

On leaving the prison Stephen Grellet went straight to Elizabeth Fry. When she heard of the plight of these prisoners she called some women Friends together to make some clothes for the children and, on the following day, delivered them to Newgate herself.

During the next four years her family responsibilities kept Elizabeth Fry at her home in the country, but she did not forget the horror of Newgate. When she returned to London she again visited the prison and insisted on going alone into the women's yard – popularly known as 'hell on earth'. She found herself in the middle of a crowd of filthy, wild, shouting, screaming, drunken women. She was not afraid and her calmness slowly calmed them. They were delighted by her willingness to hold a school for their

Elizabeth Fry at Newgate.

children. The prison governor objected, but he was no match for Elizabeth and the school was started.

The women wanted to go to the school themselves, but though this was not possible, Elizabeth Fry did organise them into groups to learn to sew and knit. The women agreed strict rules for the running of these groups, which provided for a Bible reading in the morning and evening and forbade drunkenness.

Many of the women in Newgate were awaiting transportation to Australia. There was always a riot on the night before they left, and they had to be put in irons, so that in the morning they could be herded into open wagons and driven to the river. The authorities reluctantly agreed to Elizabeth Fry's request that she and her friends should be allowed to make the arrangements for the transfer of the women to the convict ships.

On their last evening in the prison Elizabeth Fry stayed with the women, reading to them and helping them to make plans for their voyage. Early next morning Elizabeth and those helping her travelled with the women in hackney-carriages – irons and open wagons were banished. On the ship the sewing groups continued, a library was provided and, best of all, children under seven were allowed to go with their mothers. All the passengers were permitted to spend some time on deck instead of being kept below for the whole voyage. Between 1818 and 1843 Elizabeth Fry and her helpers organised all the 106 convict ships that sailed from London.

Valuable as these practical steps were to relieve the worst hardships of the prisoners, Elizabeth Fry also worked continuously at the even more important task of reforming the penal system itself.

With the story of Elizabeth Fry we have moved away from the 'quiet' period of Quaker history to the time when Friends were willing to be involved in public life. In 1833 Joseph Pease was the first Quaker to enter Parliament, to be followed later in the century by John Bright (1811–99).

QUAKERS IN SCIENCE   We can find a link between the early days of the Society and the present time in the continuing interest of Quakers in science and medicine. Friends have always been convinced that God could be found with equal vividness in the ways of nature as in their quiet Meetings for Worship. So it is not surprising that many Quakers have been Fellows of the Royal Society, which received its charter from Charles II in 1662. George Graham (1675–1751), the instrument maker, was one of the first Quakers to become a Fellow. Friends were attracted to the making of clocks and scientific instruments because the accurate work required was, for them, an expression of their religious faith. Other Quaker Fellows were botanists and naturalists. Probably the best known was John Dalton (1766–1844), the chemist who developed the atomic theory.

In modern times Quaker Fellows have included Arthur Eddington (1882–1944), the astronomer and physicist, and Kathleen Lonsdale (1903–71), the crystallographer, who was one of the first women Fellows.

TWO WORKERS FOR PEACE   My knowledge of the Quakers in this chapter (apart from Kathleen Lonsdale) comes from reading about them. But the following two were my personal friends. First, Corder Catchpool (1883–1952), who in November 1914 went to France as a member of the Friends Ambulance Unit. For the next nineteen months he witnessed the terrible carnage of the Flanders battle-fields. Corder worked tirelessly, treating the wounded and bringing comfort to the dying. Whenever possible he also tended German prisoners. He received the campaign medal, the 1914 (Mons) Star.

In March 1916 the Compulsory Service Act made service in the armed forces obligatory. Corder felt it was evil to compel men to kill others, so he resigned from the F.A.U. and became a conscientious objector. He was arrested in January 1917 and was imprisoned for over two years.

Corder's experiences at the front and in prison confirmed his deep conviction that he must work for peace. This he did for the next twenty years in England and in Germany. His first aim was to try to create a spirit of reconciliation with the German people. In the 1920s one of the ways was to help in running a food relief scheme for children and students who were starving because of the continued blockade of Germany. When the Nazis came to power in the 1930s Corder helped many Jewish and political refugees to escape. As a consequence he was himself briefly imprisoned.

In 1939 Corder and his wife were forced to return to England. He continued to work for peace in various ways: he helped aliens who had been interned, he supported conscientious objectors, and acted as a voluntary stretcher-bearer for victims of air raids. He was never afraid of taking up unpopular causes, so he campaigned energetically against the policy of obliteration bombing of German cities.

After the war Corder and his wife returned to Germany as host and hostess of a Rest Home run by Quakers for stateless people as well as German doctors, teachers and social workers who needed short holidays.

My second personal friend was Eric Baker (1920–76). His work for peace was broadly political. From 1955 to 1959 he was secretary of the National Peace Council. In the 1960s Eric Baker and other Friends secured recognition and exemption for conscientious objectors, under the terms of the Council of Europe regulations.

Perhaps Eric's most outstanding achievement was the founding, with Peter Benenson (not a Quaker), of Amnesty International in 1961. This organisation draws attention to the plight of political prisoners in all parts of the world. In connection with this work Eric became aware of the growing use of torture by governments. He first discovered the facts and then campaigned vigorously against this terrible evil in all its forms.

Eric Baker was specially interested in the problems of Cyprus, and visited the island and also Greece and Turkey several times in efforts to restore peace. Once when he was in Cyprus the Greeks and Turks started shooting at each other across the boundary that divided their territory. Eric, annoyed that a truce had been broken, marched calmly into the battle and negotiated a peace!

Corder Catchpool and Eric Baker each demonstrate that pacifists can be brave people and real peacemakers. By their ceaseless efforts these two men carried the Quaker concern for peace into modern times.

The danger of picking out famous Friends as examples of the Quaker approach to life is that it may give the impression that all Friends must be outstanding. Far from it – the great majority have lived ordinary lives and been involved in ordinary jobs. Even the famous have been very human – much as I admire Elizabeth Fry, I have to admit that she must have been rather a difficult wife to Joseph Fry! But everyone in the Society would unite in the view that it is in the quality of daily life that true religion must be expressed.

Think about . . .

How is it possible to run a successful business with the kind of ideals the Darbys had (caring for the working people, trading fairly even when rivals were making more money)? Do you think it is more difficult today?

American Quakers helped escaping slaves to reach freedom in Canada, but they were breaking the law in doing this. Were they right to disobey the law? Can you think of other laws that religious people have felt they cannot observe?

Is it right to compel people to join the armed forces in time of war? Is there any point in imprisoning conscientious objectors?

Try to find out more about the work of Amnesty International.

5

Quaker Action Today

Since we left the Friends of Winchmore Hill (several chapters ago) busily chatting away after the close of their meeting, we have explored the way Friends began, and a little of the course of their history through three centuries. This chapter is an attempt to fill in the picture of what the Society of Friends is like today.

One of the reports given among the notices after Meeting for Worship on a Sunday early in 1977 said that a letter had been sent to the Government by the Society. It urged a delay in making a decision on the construction of a fast-breeder nuclear reactor generating station. After hearing about this letter Friends in Winchmore Hill, and in all the other Quaker Meetings in the country (approximately 400), were encouraged to take action about it. This would include doing what they could to persuade local people to share the Society's concern that more careful thought should be given to the pros and cons of this source of energy.

Writing letters to the Government about

nuclear power stations may sound highly political and not the sort of thing a religious society should be doing. However, as I hope this book has made clear, Quakers don't see it this way, for they are convinced that life is a whole. So it's not possible to put religion in a box labelled 'Holy – for use on Sundays only!' For Friends, there can be no division between sacred things and secular things, and therefore political thought and actions are one aspect of religious life.

TAKING ACTION We can see how this works out in the Society of Friends today if we look briefly at the way in which that letter came to be written. In the previous months many individual Friends had been thinking a lot about the advantages and disadvantages, as well as the possible dangers, of producing and using nuclear power. Some of them shared their anxiety with other members of their local meetings who encouraged the area business meeting – the Monthly Meeting – to consider this complex question. Finally two Monthly Meetings sent minutes to Meeting for Sufferings requesting that thought should be given to this difficult and urgent subject by the whole Society. Quakers call this having 'a concern'.

At this point I must pause to explain that strange-sounding name for the Society's representative committee. The Meeting for Sufferings started in the seventeenth century as a national body, to help Friends to cope with the sufferings they endured as a result of persecution. Although Quakers long ago ceased to be persecuted, there is still so much suffering about in the world that they decided to keep the name. The consideration of nuclear generators makes the point: just think of the horrific suffering nuclear power would cause if it got out of control.

The membership of Meeting for Sufferings is made up of representatives from all the Monthly Meetings in England, Scotland and Wales. Friends in Ireland have their own organisation.

No vote is ever taken in any Quaker business meeting. Friends feel that it is better to try to reach agreement even if it means delay, rather than to allow a majority to impose its will on a minority. Friends also try to avoid scoring points off one another, for they are seeking after the truth. Their attitude to this search is helped by the fact that they think of their business meetings as a particular kind of Meeting for Worship. Of course they sometimes get heated and worked up – but it's wonderful how quickly a time of quiet will help Friends to regain their cool!

When the issue of nuclear generating stations was considered in Meeting for Sufferings there was a variety of views about the subject. It was agreed that some kind of statement should be made, and a few Friends were asked to bring a draft to a future meeting. After discussion, this document was amended and finally agreed as the view of the Society. The Clerk was authorised to send it under cover of a letter, signed by her, to the Minister for Energy. So the concern that began with individual Friends ended up on the desk of a member of the Cabinet, as the united view of the whole Society.

The concern about the right use of nuclear energy is a good example of one aspect of modern Quakerism. For the Society tries to convince other people to adopt ideas that Friends feel are right, sensible, and for the good of everyone. Meeting for Sufferings enables Friends' views on such issues to be represented nationally and internationally.

But modern Quakers also want to do things, as individuals or together, that they believe will be helpful at home and overseas. Some of these activities are best organised centrally in Friends House, the Society's headquarters in London. Other work is better done locally or by Friends abroad. Much Quaker work results from a combination of effort centrally, locally and in other lands. Meeting for Sufferings, through the appointment of committees, organises work done by the Society centrally.

Broadly, Quaker work has three main functions: to sustain the basic life of the Society, to express Quaker thought and action on social issues, and to promote Friends' concern for peace and international service. All these concerns have their roots in the history of the Society, although their expression has changed to meet modern conditions. It is unnecessary to make a long list of these activities, so here are a few examples typical of Quaker work today.

SHARING WITH OTHERS Unfortunately, the public often seems to imagine that Quakers were good people who died out with Elizabeth Fry! So the first function of Quaker work is to try to make known the existence of the Society. This is done through Quaker advertisements in the national newspapers. Many people, who thought that religion was not for them, have been delighted to discover that they

Quakers, the baby and the bathwater

Many people have 'given up religion' because in sheer honesty they cannot believe what the Christian Church seems to require them to.

They respect the 'Christian Ethic,' and they feel at heart the need for something more in living than a respectable, safe, but often dull existence. But the Church's ceremonial, the creeds, the well-loved words and customs—to some minds, these make 'religion' impossible. So they give it up, and throw the baby out with the bath-water.

If you have done this, perhaps the Quakers can help you back to an acceptance of Christianity. For these things are not religion though they can enrich it. Quaker's start with a man's—and a worshipping group's—experience of God; that is the reality behind the Christian symbols and creeds.

We find that many people who start finding out about Quaker thought discover that one idea after another clicks excitingly into place in their own personal scheme of things. You might have this same crystalising experience.

May we send you a few facts about the Society of Friends to start you thinking ? We will also, but only if wish, put you in touch with your nearest Quaker Meeting.

Part of a newspaper advertisement.

are 'natural' Quakers. Each year between two and three thousand such enquirers write to Friends House. They are sent information about the faith, worship and practice of the Society and are invited to attend their nearest Meeting for Worship if they wish to do so.

The main responsibility for maintaining local meetings as living centres of worship for a loving community of Friends rests with local members, but they can look for assistance when they need it from Friends House. This is mainly provided by publishing books, pamphlets and posters, and by arranging for Friends with special gifts and skills to lead study conferences and similar gatherings.

Children and young people need help to find their place in the Society. In most Quaker Meetings there are groups in which children can think about the beauty and complexity of God's world, and learn about the life of Jesus and how Quakers today try to put his teaching into practice. This is what the children of Winchmore Hill did when they went out of Meeting. Such groups need 'teaching' material and this is also available from Friends House. Summer schools for young people are held in various parts of the country, and a national Junior Yearly Meeting takes place once a year. The upper age range of young people arrange their own activities, and publish a monthly magazine called *Young Quaker*.

SOCIAL CONCERN The second aspect of Quaker work is concerned with Friends' attitudes to social problems. The first thing to say about this is that a large number of Friends choose to work in various branches of medicine, education, and the social and probation services etc. The second point to note is that the actual amount of direct social work organised by the Society is relatively small compared with that done by some other religious bodies. This is deliberate policy. Friends are willing to meet a need when they see it, especially if no one else is doing anything about it. However, they do not feel that the Society should assume responsibility for too many large projects. So, having shown how the need can be met, Quakers generally like to pass the work over to a body better able to deal with it, such as a local authority.

It has been said that the Society of Friends is the one religious body where it's respectable to have been in prison! Earlier chapters have shown that Quakers had ample opportunity to know what it was like to be 'inside'. In the twentieth century many Quakers have been imprisoned as conscientious objectors during two world wars. So modern experience has kept alive an interest in prisoners and for the reform of the penal system. Quaker 'Ministers' are still appointed to visit prisons.

Friends have long had a particular interest in helping ex-prisoners. A good example of this today is a venture sponsored by the Liverpool Quaker Penal Affairs Group. This is a house which provides ex-offenders with a unique combination of a bed-sitter and hostel to which they can go on leaving prison. In the house they can find both privacy and companionship. The object of the venture is to help the men to re-establish themselves in the community.

In the eighteenth century William Tuke of York was shocked by the terrible treatment meted out to people thought to be mad, who were frequently put in chains. Tuke believed that insanity was just another form of illness, and that sufferers should be given kindness, sympathy and understanding. So in 1790 he started the Retreat in York, which was the first mental hospital, as opposed to a lunatic asylum. It is still run by Quakers today for the treatment of people suffering from mental illness.

The Society became involved in the care of elderly people in the early part of the Second World War. It was realised that there were many old people living in areas likely to be bombed, who had no one to help them and nowhere to go. Many of our country Meeting Houses were immediately turned into old people's homes until we could find more suitable accommodation. However, Quakers felt that the care of the elderly was really the job of local authorities. So most of these homes were handed over to them, although a few were kept for our use. Today the Quaker Housing Trust assists in the building of accommodation suitable for the elderly.

Thankfully, slavery has almost disappeared from the world, so Friends' attention has now turned to the problem of community relations. Members of the Society are asked 'Do you behave with brotherly love to all men whatever their race, background or opinion?' As a small practical contribution an inter-faith exhibition is promoted. This seeks to help people to appreciate the different kinds of worship that are practised in modern Britain.

Ever since the time of George Fox, Friends have been keenly interested in education, not just as a means of preparing people to earn their living, but as a way of helping them to develop all their gifts as fully as possible. Today there are nine Quaker boarding schools: six are coeducational, two are mainly for boys and one is for girls. Staff and pupils are not limited to Friends – in fact non-Friends greatly outnumber Friends. But many Quakers choose to send their children to state schools and many Quaker teachers like to teach in them.

One of the most interesting experiments in thinking about social questions in recent years was the result of the work of an unofficial group of Friends who, in 1963, wrote an essay called *Towards a Quaker View of Sex*. The group was mainly concerned about the negative view most people took of homosexuals and they wanted everyone to think freshly about sex as part of the total relationship between people, in which they would act towards each other with love, care and trust.

WORK OVERSEAS The third function of Quaker work is largely concerned with service overseas. In the past Quakers have done missionary work, especially in education and medicine, though in recent years Friends have been less keen on missionary activity. Probably this lack of missionary zeal stems from the fact that Quakers tend to be all too anxious to see the other person's point of view rather than trying to convert people to their way of thinking.

A lot of Friends go to developing countries as doctors, nurses and technicians of various kinds, either employed by the government of the country, or as members of a Quaker Service team. For instance, drought forced the Somali nomads of Ethiopia to adopt a new way of life. They needed to learn how to irrigate the land so that they could grow crops and rear cattle. Irrigation requires pumps and pumps need a mechanic to maintain them. So a Quaker mechanic was sent there to teach the people how to use pumps and other equipment. This is just one example of Quaker service today.

WORKING FOR PEACE   A different kind of interest is the work towards understanding and reconciliation between nations. Quaker House in New York is one of the channels through which this is carried out. Diplomats visiting the United Nations are always welcomed there. During the meetings of the Assembly, Quakers have a small international team of Friends in residence. They seek to be of help to people working in the United Nations, and give special encouragement to members of delegations who are sponsoring any unpopular cause with which Friends feel sympathy.

This is one of the ways of expressing the Quaker concern for peace and the abolition of war. Friends in this country are anxious to make the public aware of the urgent need for disarmament, because of the enormous amount of money spent on arms, by Britain in particular and by most nations in general. Quakers also feel that the more arms stocks are built up, the greater is the danger of causing the war they are supposed to prevent.

There are many ways of creating better relations between nations and easing tensions; we will take two areas to which

Friends have contributed. One is their efforts to help ease the terrible situation in Northern Ireland. The fact that there has always been just one Quaker organisation for the whole of Ireland has been a helpful starting-point. In Northern Ireland itself Friends have tried to do all they can to encourage communication and understanding between people who hold opposing views. A practical step has been the provision of comforts for the families visiting their relatives in prison. There is also a Quaker minibus operating in areas where public transport is impossible.

Another experimental area of Friends' activities is with work camps. Quakers run several of these each year. A recent one was held for two weeks in the summer. Fifteen young people from eight nations, including Britain, worked voluntarily, building a chicken run and a goat pen and

Young people from Britain, Germany and Bangladesh at a Quaker work camp, clearing a play area in Hackney.

clearing the garden in the grounds of a community for mentally handicapped adults. Accommodation for the campers was in a barn in the grounds. The group worked from 9 a.m. to 5 p.m., with a day off for every three days of work. In their leisure time the campers achieved another of their aims, which was to make friends with members of the community. This they did through folk dancing, a barbecue and games of rounders.

Work camps provide opportunities for an international group of young people to know one another and to understand the people among whom they work. Camps also achieve work that otherwise would not be done. They are an example of one way in which the Society of Friends seeks to witness to its convictions and to be of service to others.

Think about . . .

How far do you think a Church should take political action? What action do you think religious people might suitably take?

How far do you think it is right for a religious body to seek to persuade other people to adopt its ideas?

What in your view is the case for traditional missionary work, and what is the case against it?

How would you answer the question 'Do you behave with brotherly love to all men whatever their race, background or opinion?'

Quakers think that disarmament is essential if nations are to avoid war. Do you agree with them?

6

Running the Society

YEARLY MEETING   Once a year every member of the Society may attend and participate in London Yearly Meeting. This is the final policy- and decision-making body for Friends in England, Scotland and Wales. Friends in Ireland have their own Yearly Meeting.

One of the important jobs of Yearly Meeting is to revise, at roughly twenty-five-year intervals, the *Book of Christian Discipline*. This is in two parts: 'Christian Faith and Practice in the Experience of the Society of Friends', and 'Church Government'. The purpose of the whole book is clearly indicated by the titles of the two sections. The first outlines the sort of things that Quakers believe and do, by describing the way that Friends in the past and present have tried to live, and the convictions that have drawn them together as a religious society. The second part outlines the way that Friends have agreed to run the Society. It also contains the 'Advices and Queries', which give one of the best pictures of Quakerism.

There are twenty-three 'Queries' from which two may be quoted to give you some idea of their approach. The third asks:

> Is your religion rooted in personal experience of God? How does it find expression in your life?

The twentieth asks:

> Are you working towards the removal of social injustices? Have you attempted to examine their causes objectively, and are you ready to abandon old prejudices and think again? Do you, as disciples of Christ, take a living interest in the social conditions of the district in which you live? Do you seek to promote the welfare of those in any kind of need, and a just distribution of the resources of the world?

The *Book of Christian Discipline* is not issued as a set of beliefs, rules and regulations which every member must accept, but rather as guidelines to faith and life. Nevertheless, its authority rests in the fact that it has been drawn up by the whole Society, and is regularly revised and kept up to date.

MONTHLY MEETINGS   Enough has been said to indicate the significance of Yearly Meeting (and of its representative committee, Meeting for Sufferings) for Quakers today. But the chief focus of the life and work of the Society is in its Monthly Meetings, of which there are seventy-two. These Monthly Meetings cover a wide area, and usually draw together a number of Preparative Meetings. These deal with the 'business' of the local Friends Meeting. Winchmore Hill Meeting is one of five Preparative (local) Meetings that make up Devonshire House and Tottenham Monthly (Area) Meeting.

Among the many important powers they have is that of admitting people into membership, which is not just a formality but the sign of a particular relationship between the whole Society and the individual. Many of the enquirers who reply to press advertisements eventually ask to become members after they have attended a Meeting for Worship for some time. The Monthly Meeting asks two Friends to talk with the applicant. If, during this conversation, it becomes obvious that a real link exists between the person asking for membership and the Society, then the Monthly Meeting recognises this as a fact by recording it in its minutes. The signs of such a relationship include the knowledge that Quaker worship is helpful to the applicant, and that he is in general sympathy with the outlook of the Society.

Monthly Meeting also appoints men and women Friends to fill a number of offices in the Society. Elders are appointed to have a special care for the spiritual life of Friends in their meetings, while Overseers see that practical jobs like visiting people when they are ill are not forgotten.

MARRIAGE Another appointment made by the Monthly Meeting is that of the Registering Officer to be responsible for the arrangements of Quaker weddings. Since the seventeenth century, when Quakers refused to be married before a priest or minister, Friends have been able to solemnise the marriages of their members. The procedure is very simple once the Registering Officer is satisfied that all the necessary information is available, and that public notice of the proposed marriage has been made.

A special Meeting for Worship is held, during which the couple make a mutual promise of faithfulness to each other. First the man says 'Friends, I take this my Friend (naming her) to be my wife, promising through divine assistance, to be unto her a loving and faithful husband, so long as we both on earth shall live.' Then the woman makes a promise in similar terms 'to be a loving and faithful wife'.

The Meeting then continues for about half an hour. Towards its close the Registering Officer reads a certificate that records the actual promises made. This is signed by

A Quaker wedding.

the man and woman, and is witnessed by a few people present. Later all who have heard the promise made are invited to add their signatures: with so many witnesses it would be difficult for anyone to deny that the couple were truly married. The Registering Officer also has power to issue a State certificate of marriage.

In common with all religious bodies, Friends dislike divorce, not least because of the suffering that it inevitably causes. But they recognise that mistakes can be made, and after every effort at reconciliation has been tried and failed, they believe that the fact that the marriage has finally broken down must be accepted. Quakers are also willing, in special cases, to allow divorced people to be remarried in a Quaker wedding.

MEETING HOUSES   Another important responsibility of the Monthly Meeting is the care of all the Meeting Houses in its area. In the opening chapter I described the one at Winchmore Hill, but they come in a great variety of shapes and sizes. Those that were built in the seventeenth and eighteenth centuries are very beautiful and many are still in use. Those erected in the period between the mid-nineteenth and early twentieth centuries are sometimes not so attractive. But Meeting House design has improved greatly as the years have passed and we now have some very exciting modern buildings.

Quite a few Meetings use converted houses or other premises. It is our aim to use all our buildings for a variety of purposes in addition to Meetings for Worship. One great advantage of the Quaker Meeting is that it does not need a special or consecrated building – it can be held anywhere, in a private house, a community hall or any place where people can gather.

WORSHIP More important than the buildings is what happens inside them. The central activity is the Meeting for Worship in which everyone plays an equal part. I asked a member of my meeting why she became a Friend. She replied: 'I go to meeting because being quiet with other people helps me to love them even though I don't always like the things they do.' She added: 'Loving and trusting people is often difficult – but that's what Quakers think real religion enables you to achieve.'

In writing of Quaker worship nothing has been said about Holy Communion or Baptism, for the simple reason that Quakers do not use these outward sacraments. For Friends Jesus is, by his spirit, present in our Meetings for Worship. Children, we believe, grow into the loving communion of a Friends Meeting by being accepted as persons in their own right. If they wish, Quaker parents can ask for their children to be made members at birth. Most parents prefer to register their children as 'attenders', and allow them to make up their own minds about membership when they grow up.

The Meeting House is not only the place where worship takes place; it is also the focus of the life of the local community of Friends. A useful tradition that has come down from the seventeenth century is the way in which we address one another, as it helps to emphasise the fact that everyone is expected to be friendly, and is equally involved in the life of the Society. We do not use titles, and no one would dream of calling me 'Mr Gorman', which would be far too formal for a friendly society. Instead they would say 'George Gorman', although in practice most would call me 'George' as the use of first names only is becoming widely accepted. When starting a letter we write 'Dear Friend', if we do not know the person, or 'Dear John Brown', if we do.

SHARING TOGETHER   One happy thing is that the warm sense of belonging that I know in my own Meeting can be discovered throughout the world family of Friends. It is true even of those Meetings in America which are so unlike those in this country – they have Quaker churches, pastors and a programmed form of worship.

In the early days of the Society, Friends thought of themselves, rather arrogantly, as 'primitive Christianity revived'. Today we respect the witness of other Christians and value our warm relations with them. We are glad to share in the work of the British Council of Churches as associate members, and many Meetings are involved in local Councils of Churches. Many individual Friends gain great benefit from the outlook and experience of non-Christian religions, especially those of the East, and in particular from some forms of Buddhism.

In this book I have tried to give a general impression of the Society of Friends in the past and the present as I understand it. It is a Religious Society of Friends in which people may know, care for and love one another. It is not, however, a community shut in on itself, for its aim is to be of service to others. Our Society is deeply concerned with the search for truth. This cannot be separated from the truth about people. One of the most important ways of finding God is through our experience of relationships with people. The New Testament tells us that 'God is love' – if we are going to know this love ourselves, we shall find it as we love and are loved by others.

On a Sunday morning some time ago Winchmore Hill Quakers had settled into their quiet meeting, although as I recall it, the silence wasn't very deep, when something happened to change it to a most profound silence. A woman Friend spoke about a recent visit to hospital when she had been told that she had about six months to live. She didn't want Friends to be sentimental, as she was determined to make the best of the brief time left to her, and she asked for their help. She knew that they would support her family by their loving care when she died.

In the deep silence that followed her words we all knew that we were experiencing the fact that love cannot be destroyed by death. We had the marvellous sense that we were transported to a new level of living not affected by time and space. It was an experience that gave us all the courage to face both life and death.

Think about . . .

What kind of answers would you give to the two 'Queries' on p. 56?

How effective do you think is the Quaker method of conducting the business meetings of the Society?

Why do you think people want to go to church?

What kind of difference do you think that religion should make to people's lives?

Important Dates

1624–91 Life of George Fox.
1642   Beginning of Civil War.
1643   George Fox leaves home.
1644–
  –1718 Life of William Penn.
1649   Execution of Charles I.
1652   George Fox at Pendle Hill, Brigflatts and Swarthmore Hall.
1660   Restoration of Charles II.
1661–2   4200 Quakers in prison.
1667–9   Monthly Meetings established.
1682   William Penn sails for America.
1709   Smelting of iron by Darby.
1720–72 Life of John Woolman.
1780–
  –1845 Life of Elizabeth Fry.
1790   Founding of The Retreat, York.
1833   First Quaker Member of Parliament.
1870   Friends undertake relief work in Franco-Prussian War.
1914   Friends Ambulance Unit established.
1920   First World Conference of Friends.
1937   Second World Conference of Friends.
1939   Large-scale relief work (World War II).
1951   Quaker mission to Russia.
1952   Third World Conference of Friends.
1955   Quaker mission to China.
1961   Founding of Amnesty International.
1967   Fourth World Conference of Friends.

Further Reading

George Gorman has also written:

Introducing Quakers (F.H.S.C.). A popular introduction to the Society of Friends.

The Amazing Fact of Quaker Worship (F.H.S.C.).

OTHER WORKS

Advices and Queries (London Yearly Meeting). A brief 'official' summary of Quaker views.

Christian Faith and Practice (London Yearly Meeting). The Society's corporately accepted account of its worship, faith and practice.

Corder Catchpool by JEAN GREAVES (F.H.S.C. 1953).

The Discovery of Quakerism by HAROLD LOUKES (F.H.S.C. 1970). A lucid account of Quaker history and faith, written for sixth formers in Friends' schools.

George Fox by VERNON NOBLE (F.H.S.C. 1969).

Meet the Quakers (F.H.S.C.). An illustrated and informative brochure.

Quaker by Convincement by GEOFFREY HUBBARD (Penguin 1974). A comprehensive book for general readers.

Quakerism — A Faith to Live By by ELFRIDA VIPONT (Friends Book Centre). A picture of Quakerism as seen in the lives of Friends throughout their history.

William Penn by VERNON NOBLE (F.H.S.C. 1971).

You and the Quakers by ALISON SHARMAN (F.H.S.C. 1977). A lively short book for young people with amusing cartoons by Michael Ricketts.

Young Person's Guide to the Quakers (F.H.S.C.). An illustrated and informative brochure.

Useful Addresses

Friends House, Euston Road, London NW1 2BJ.
All the following are based at the address above:

Friends Book Centre can supply books, pamphlets and posters, and can provide material for children's classes.

Children's and Young People's Committee can provide teaching aids and class material.

Work Camps Committee is the source for all information about work camps.

Friends Home Service Committee will be glad to answer questions from people who are wondering whether Quakerism is for them, and provide general information about the Society.